THE HOW AND WHY WONDER® BOOK OF
WEATHER

By George Bonsall
Illustrated by George Pay

Edited under the supervision of
Dr. Paul E. Blackwood
Washington, D. C.

Text and illustrations approved by

Oakes A. White
Brooklyn Children's Museum
Brooklyn, New York

PRICE/STERN/SLOAN
Publishers, Inc., Los Angeles
1983

INTRODUCTION

This *How and Why Wonder® Book* deals with a subject that is important to everyone, for in many ways weather rules the life of man. And like the others in the *How and Why Wonder® Book* series, this one answers dozens of basic questions about an area of knowledge in which scientists are constantly exploring. So this book is of interest to science-minded children and their parents. It explains how air, sun and water intermingle in a thousand different ways to produce an ever-changing yet predictable weather pattern.

The *How and Why Wonder® Books* not only give accurate information about scientific subjects, but they also explain the various ways in which scientists explore and investigate the universe. The experiment is one of these ways. And this book emphasizes experiments. It suggests dozens of simple activities which young readers will want to try. Doing the experiments is a way of practicing one of the most important methods used by scientists to get accurate information about the environment.

If you have ever wondered about snow or fog, hurricanes or tornadoes, the seasons, or any other topic concerning weather, you will find much helpful information and colorful pictures in these pages.

Paul E. Blackwood

Dr. Blackwood is a professional employee in the U. S. Office of Education. This book was edited by him in his private capacity and no official support or endorsement by the Office of Education is intended or should be inferred.

CONTENTS

WEATHER

What makes weather?

WHY DOES the earth have a variety of seasons and climate, while the moon does not? The answer is — weather.

Clouds, wind, rain and snow — these are some of the things we can see or feel as signs of what we call weather.

You may have sometimes wondered why it is that weather conditions are constantly changing. Wind, temperature, air pressure and moisture are the factors responsible. When air moves from place to place at varying rates of speed, we call it the wind. As it moves, it may carry warm air, cool air, dry air or moist air. Air temperature really affects weather more than anything else, and this is largely determined by the sun. (The sun sends its energy into our atmosphere, where it is absorbed and transformed into heat.) High-pressure areas, created by cold air, generally indicate fair weather. Low-pressure areas are created by warm air (which weighs less than cold air) and generally indicate cloudy or stormy weather. Moving air (winds) usually follows a route going from a high-pressure area to a low-pressure area. Moisture in the air is simply water vapor, but it may take the form of rain, sleet, snow, fog, clouds or measurable humidity.

Sun + Air + Water = Weather

Summer is the warmest season of the year. It is a time when the sun shines most directly over the land. In the United States, summer includes the months of June, July and August, a time of the year when many people go to the seashore.

The season between summer and winter is autumn. It includes the months of September, October and November. It is the time of year when leaves fall from the trees, and so autumn is often called fall.

Is there weather on the moon? But the moon is lighted and warmed by the sun. Why doesn't the moon have clouds and rain and wind and snow? The moon has neither air nor water, so there can be no weather on the moon.

Winter is the coldest season of the year. In the United States, it includes the months of December, January and February, a time of the year when children like to ice-skate, go sledding and play in the snow.

THE AIR ON TOP OF YOUR HEAD

Can you see air?

WHAT do you know about this ocean of air you live in? Do you breathe it? Can you see through it? Do you feel it when it moves? The answer is yes. But it's hard to picture something you can't see. It's hard to believe something is real if you can't look at it and touch it. Are there ways of showing that air is real?

When you turn a glass upside down and push it into water, no water will go into the glass. The air in the glass keeps the water from coming in, which shows that air takes up space.

Does air take up space?

You might try turning a glass upside down and pushing it straight down into a bowl of water. There is something which keeps the water from filling the glass — isn't there? You thought the glass was empty. It wasn't filled with something to drink, but it was full. The glass was full of air. Only real things take up space. Air and water can't fit into the same glass any more than you and a friend can fit into the same clothes at the same time. The water can't get in the glass unless you tilt it to one side and let some of the air out.

Is air real?

Next try blowing up a balloon. When you pinch it, what do you feel inside? The only thing you put into the balloon was air. It must be air that you feel. If you feel the air, then the air is there. The air is real.

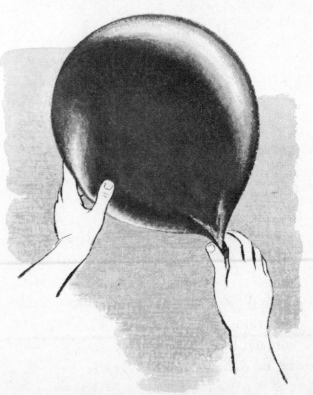

You can actually feel air by pressing on a blown-up balloon. This shows that air is real.

Is air heavy?

How much does air weigh? It depends on when and where you measure it. The air in your living room may weigh as much as you do. Right now there is a column of air resting on your head and shoulders which is several hundred miles high. It weighs hundreds of pounds. How can you support such a weight? You couldn't bear it at all if the same air pressure in your body didn't also push in the opposite direction. The experiment described below, and illustrated on the right, helps to explain this idea.

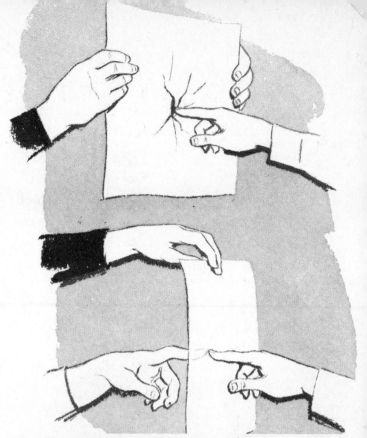

Air has weight and presses down on us. However, the pressure in our bodies is equal to the air pressing down on us, so we don't feel the weight of the air.

Does air push in all directions?

Ask someone to hold a thin piece of paper in both hands. Now push your finger against one side of the paper. You've poked a hole right through. Take another piece of paper. This time use a finger on each hand. Push at the same spot from each side of the paper. Nothing happens. The pressure is equal on both sides of the paper. So, too, the pressure of air in your body is equal to the pressure of that column of air resting on your head and shoulders.

You can squeeze air, as this experiment with a hand pump shows.

Can you squeeze water?

The tall column of air presses down on your head the way a tall column of water presses down on a deep-sea diver. But there is one big difference between these columns. You cannot squeeze water.

Can you squeeze air?

But you squeeze air every time you use a pump to blow up a basketball. If you held your finger over the end of the pump, it would be harder to push the handle, but you could at least push it part way.

AIR PRESSES DOWN

Does air press down?

SUPPOSE you had a stack of pancakes three feet high. Each of the pancakes weighs something. Each is pressed down by the total weight of all the pancakes on top of it. The bottom pancakes would be squeezed the most. The top pancakes would be squeezed the least. But you would get more to eat if you took a two-inch stack of pancakes from the bottom of the pile than you would if you helped yourself to a two-inch stack from the top. Air is like these pancakes.

Air is made up of tiny bits called molecules. More than a *trillion* of these molecules could fit in a space the size of the head of a pin! They squeeze one another like the stack of pancakes, so the greatest number of molecules is found in a layer very close to the earth.

Helium is used to inflate balloons and airships, which then rise in the air. The higher up you go, the thinner and lighter is the air.

Is air lighter on a mountain or in a valley?

Up in the mountains and high in the sky, the air becomes thinner. The molecules are farther apart. (The pancakes were farther apart on top of the stack.) Way up high, the air is so thin that mountain climbers and pilots must wear oxygen masks to breathe.

You have seen balloons filled with a gas called helium. Helium is much lighter than air. When the lighter-than-air balloon leaves the ground, it rises through the thick layer of air like a cork rising in a tank of water. But the balloon cannot keep rising forever. After it has risen a few miles, the air becomes so light and thin that the balloon is no longer lighter than the air.

Why is it colder on a mountain than in a valley?

Something else happens when you climb high mountains or fly in the sky. You get colder. There are many mountains in the world which have snow on their peaks all year round. This is because our ocean of air is graduated from heavy layers to very thin layers as we get farther from sea level. High up the air is thinner, lighter and colder because molecules are farther apart.

If you were to take temperature readings of the air as you climbed a mountain, you would find that the higher you went, the colder it would get.

Does rubbing make things hotter?

Close to earth the molecules are all squeezed together. They are restless. They push and shove harder and harder. As they rub against one another they become hotter. So it is possible for you to see two different effects of air pressure in the same part of the country — snow on a mountaintop, where the air is thin and molecules are far apart, and flowers growing in a warm valley beneath, where molecules of air have been squeezed tightly together and heated up.

Feel the molecules which make up your skin become hotter when you rub your palms together very quickly.

Feel the side of a hand pump just after it has been used. It is warm. The molecules have been squeezed together.

HEATING BY DAY— COOLING BY NIGHT

Dark-colored things hold on to heat from the sun's rays better than light-colored things. For this reason, many people wear white garments in the summertime, since white absorbs less heat from the sun than darker colors.

Why do you wear light-colored clothing in summer? IN THE winter you wear warm clothes to protect you from the cold. Most of these clothes are dark-colored — dark reds, navy blues, deep greens. In the summer, when you wear fewer clothes, these clothes are often of white or pale colors. Why? The answer is in the sun's rays.

Try putting a piece of white paper in the sun. Next to it put a piece of black paper. After a few minutes the black paper will feel warmer than the white paper. Things which are dark-colored absorb more of the sun's rays and produce more heat than light-colored things. The dark clothing keeps you warmer in the winter time. It holds on to the heat from the sun's rays. The light-colored clothing you wear in summer helps keep you cool. It does not absorb as much heat from the sun.

If you put the piece of black paper in the sun again and feel it two minutes later, five minutes later, and ten minutes later, you can feel it getting warmer. It gets warmer because the sun shines on it for a longer time. Your skin feels the same way the longer you lie out in the sun. It gets warmer and warmer.

When does the earth cool off best? The same thing that happens to you in the sun happens to the rocks and soil and water on earth. The longer the sun's rays shine upon them, the hotter they become. The earth grows warmer by day. At night, when the sun is gone, the earth cools off.

WINTER

EACH of the four seasons in our northern hemisphere wears its own face. So it is as easy to tell them apart as it is for you to recognize each of your friends. Each season has its own weather. Each weather change makes a change in you. How does winter's face look? How can you tell when the winter season is coming?

Is a winter day longer or shorter than a winter night?

The days grow much shorter and the nights grow very long. The wind blows colder. The sun doesn't seem to be as warm. The season is changing. You're changing, too. You're changing into heavier clothes which protect you from the cold. You're changing the games you play and the food you eat. You're beginning to spend more time indoors. What happens when winter finally comes?

In winter the days are shorter and the nights are longer than at any other time of year. The sun rises later, after you are up and dressed. It sets at night before suppertime. The soil and the rocks and the water are warmed by the sun during the short day and have much time to cool during the long night.

Why do the sun's rays give less heat in winter? Even when the sun is shining, it does not heat the soil and the rocks and the water during the winter months as much as it does at other times of the year. As you watch the sun cross the sky, you'll notice that it is not as high as at other seasons of the year. The position of the sun in the winter sky causes the sun's rays to strike the earth at a slant.

If you pretend that a flashlight is the sun and shine it down on a table at a slant, you will see that the light is spread over a much larger area than it is when you shine the flashlight straight down. The sun's light hits the earth at a wide slant during the winter. It is spread over a wider area and does not give as much heat as it does when its rays shine straight down.

During the summer, the sun's rays shine directly down. In the winter, the rays are slanted.

SPRING

JUST as you are beginning to feel that winter will never end, things begin to happen which tell you it will. A warm breeze blows across an open field. Large cracks appear in the ice on the skating pond. Rivers and streams swell and overflow with melting snow.

Changes happen to you, too. You take off the extra sweaters under your coat. Your nose and hands and feet don't get as cold when you play outside. You spend more time outdoors. All these signs and changes mean something. Spring is coming!

Do days become longer in spring? 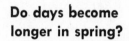 What sort of face does spring have? The days of spring grow longer and the nights grow shorter. One day, about March 21, the day and night are exactly the same length. Now the sun has more time to heat up the soil and the rocks and the water. It melts away the snow and ice. It begins to warm the seeds planted deep in the soil on farms, in gardens, in the meadows and woods.

The spring sun climbs higher in the sky. Its rays strike the earth at less of a slant than in winter. They give more heat to the area on which they fall. But they are still falling at a slant and if you turn your face up to the sun so its rays strike you more directly, you will discover that you feel warmer.

Why do blossoms twist toward the sun? You learned this from the flowers which turn during the day to follow the sun. Spring blossoms stretch and twist upward in the direction of the sun's rays to get more direct heat.

Robin redbreast and new green leaves on the trees are signs of spring.

SUMMER

When do we have our longest days and shortest nights?

SOMETIMES so quietly you hardly know it has come, summer arrives. Just as winter and spring have their signals, so summer has its signals. What do you see when you look for the face of summer?

You see that the days are longer than at any other time of year. The sun shines in your eyes in the morning and wakes you up. It sets long after supper and the nights are short.

You take off jackets and heavy socks and put on light clothing. You eat more cold foods and drink cool drinks. You enjoy games that you can only enjoy in the hot weather. You swim outdoors and you go boating.

Summer is here!

In the summer, the path of the sun is longer and farther to the north than the sun's winter path. The path of the sun on June 22 is longer than on any other day, which makes June 22 the longest day in the year.

Does the summer sun rise high?

What happens to our sun in the summer? It crosses the sky higher than at any other time of the year. Its rays bring more heat to the earth. They are direct rays and shine on a smaller area. These rays strike the earth for more hours each day. The short nights of summer mean less time for the earth to cool before the sun rises and begins its job of heating all over again the next day.

You can understand from the experiment pictured here one reason why the earth grows so warm in summer. Two pieces of black paper have been cut the same size, with pieces of cardboard placed behind them to keep them stiff. One piece is laid flat on the ground so that the sun shines on it directly. The other is propped up so that the sun strikes it at a slant. After a few minutes the black paper which is flat on the ground becomes warmer than the piece which is propped up. In the same way, the earth is made warmer by the summer sun's more direct rays than by the more slanting rays of the other seasons. You might try this experiment yourself, though it may be hard to tell the difference in temperature unless conditions are ideal.

The rocks and the soil and the water on earth, like the paper you placed in the sun, are being heated for a longer time during the long summer days. They become hotter and hotter.

In the summer, direct rays of the sun strike the earth. This experiment will show that the earth is made warmer by direct rays than by the slanted rays of the sun in other seasons of the year.

In the fall, the path of the sun across the sky becomes shorter than it was in the summer. The days become shorter and the nights become longer. Note the sun's journey across the sky.

FALL

Do days get shorter in the fall? ONE DAY, in September, you will notice that the days are getting a little cooler. The winds are brisk. You put on a sweater when you go out to play. After a summer of salads and cool drinks, you enjoy eating a bowl of hot soup. Is it your imagination or is the sun setting a little earlier? It isn't your imagination. The sun is beginning to make a shorter journey across the sky each day. There are fewer hours of heating. The nights grow a little longer. There are more hours of cooling. You can see that the sun is not quite so high in the sky as it was in summer. The sun's rays strike the earth at more of a slant and lose some of their heating power.

About September 21, there comes another date when the length of the day is exactly the same as the length of the night.

Soon you notice the leaves of the trees changing colors and falling to the ground. They blow about in the wind. The flowers and fruits and vegetables of summer are gone. This is the face of fall.

What causes changes in seasons? You have lived through four seasons, four different weather patterns, four changes in the way you dress, the games you play, sometimes even the kind of house you live in. All these changes were made because of the weather.

Are you ready to start another year? Will you know when winter is coming?

HOTTER IS FASTER

This experiment, using talcum powder and an electric light bulb, shows that hot air rises. When air is heated, it expands and gets lighter.

Does hot air rise?

WHAT happens when air is heated?

An electric light bulb which has been burning a few minutes heats the air above it and causes that air to rise. If you sprinkle a tiny amount of talcum powder or corn starch into the air a few inches above the bulb, you can watch as the powdered air is pushed upward.

Have you ever watched a coal-burning fire? If there is no strong current of air, smoke goes straight up. What we see are bits of black carbon, which will settle down later as soot. Smoke rises because the air has been heated. Hot air is lighter than cold air. It rises like the lighter-than-air balloon.

What happens to air when it is heated?

Something else happens when air is heated. The tiny particles, or molecules of which air is made, begin to move about faster and faster. As they bump one another harder and harder, they move farther apart. They take up more room. You can watch this happen. Measure around the largest part of a balloon with a tape measure or piece of thread. Then place the balloon in the bright sun. After a few minutes, measure it again and you will see that the balloon is larger. It has the same weight of air inside, but it takes up more space. So we know that air which is heated not only rises, but it also expands.

AN AIR EXCHANGE

Does cold air move?

A HOT radiator is a good thing to stir up the air molecules. As the air near the radiator is heated, it rises. Cold air sweeps in to take its place. This cold air is heated by the radiator and it rises. More cold air rushes in. This is how air keeps moving or circulating about in the room. The warm air is pushed away by the cold air. When the cold air becomes warm, it rises and more cold air moves in. This goes on and on, around and around, indefinitely.

Where is the warmest part of a room?

So you would expect to find the temperature of the room higher near the ceiling than near the floor. If you let fresh air into the room by opening the window both top and bottom, the cool air coming in at the bottom will push warm air out at the top.

You can watch this happen. Fasten paper strips to parts of a window, as shown in the illustration. Watch the directions in which the air moves the paper strips. The strips at the top will move out as warm air is pushed out. The strips at the bottom will move in as cold air rushes in.

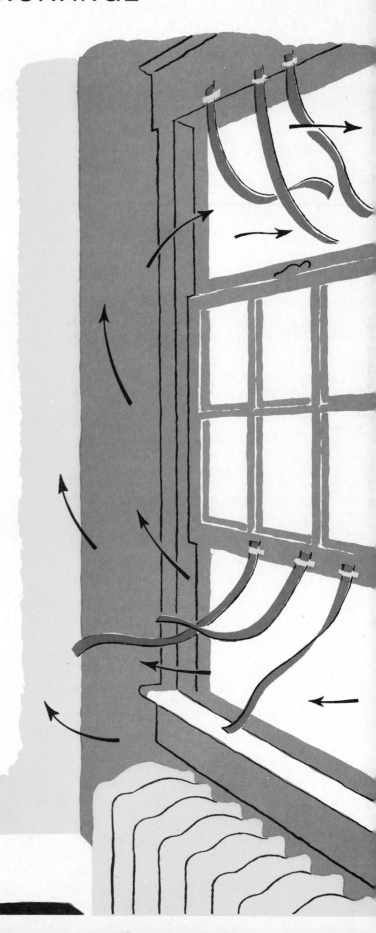

Warm air rises, but as it rises, it is replaced by cooler air. This experiment, using paper strips fastened to parts of a window, shows this idea.

A TINY TORNADO

Does the earth heat evenly?

AIR circulates in the room because of a difference in temperature. Winds blow outdoors for the same reason. All day long the rays of the sun shoot through space and through the earth's ocean of air, striking the soil, rocks and water. As the soil, rocks and water are heated, they heat the layer of air nearest to them. Do they heat it evenly? No. By placing black and white papers in the sun, you showed that darker materials heat faster than lighter materials.

This picture-diagram shows, on a very small scale, how a tornado takes place. Warm air rises; cold air comes in to take its place. As the cold air moves in, it picks up objects in its path and whirls them about as a tornado might do.

When does air move fastest?

Some areas of the earth are lighter than others and will absorb fewer of the sun's rays. Asphalt is dark, so a hot asphalt driveway will make the air above it very warm. As the warm air rises, the cool air from a shady spot next to it will rush in to take its place. As the air rushes in quickly, it will pick up leaves and papers in its path and whirl them about like a top. What is happening is a miniature version of a violent storm called a tornado. The greater the difference in temperature, the quicker the air will move.

WHY BREEZES BLOW

Why does wind blow?

SOIL and rock heat much faster than water. Put some cool earth in a saucer and some water in another saucer and see how this works. Put both saucers in the sun. In about half an hour the surface of the soil will feel warm, but the water will still feel cool. Test the temperature with a thermometer.

Water doesn't heat as rapidly as the earth. When warm air over the land rises, the cooler air over the water comes in to take its place. This creates an onshore breeze, and as you know, it's much cooler nearer a lake or the ocean than the city.

Like the soil in the saucer, the land is heated by the sun and it becomes warmer than the water. The land heats the air above it and this warm air rises. Cooler air from nearby water moves in to take its place and creates a movement of air called an onshore breeze.

When the sun goes down, the land cools off. The water is now warmer than the land and warms the air above it. The warm air over the water begins to rise. Cooler air from over the land moves out to take its place. This movement of air is called an offshore breeze.

During the day, it is the land which *heats* faster than the water. But when the sun goes down, it is the land that also *cools* faster than the water. When the warmer air over the water rises, the cooler air from the land rushes in to take its place. This creates an offshore breeze.

Do winds change direction? At night things change. Soil and rock, which heat faster than water, cool off faster than water. If you remove the top layer from the saucer of soil, you will find the soil that is left is still cool. The water is also cool, but not much cooler down deep than on the surface. The rays of the sun only hit the surface of soil and rock. The same rays go deep into water and heat it to a depth of several feet.

WATER YOU CAN'T SEE

What happens when water "dries up"?

WHEN we say that a pond has dried up we mean that the water in it has disappeared. What happened to it? The tiny bits or molecules which make up water have jumped into the air and are bouncing and bumping about with the molecules of air. We say the pond water has *evaporated* and we call water carried by the air "water vapor." The amount of water in the air varies at different times, but there is probably a quart or more of water in the air in your bedroom.

This picture illustrates evaporation taking place in a pond. The water is "drying up." Actually, the molecules of water bounce up toward the sky. The water carried along by the air is called water vapor.

Water will evaporate faster when it is exposed to the sun than when it is placed in the shade.

quickly than a wet piece placed where the air is still. When you try this, it is best to wet one piece of paper and tear it in half so that one piece is just as wet as the other.

More water will evaporate from a large surface than a small one. A saucer with a spoonful of water spread over its bottom will dry up faster than the same amount of water left in the spoon.

Water evaporates more quickly when the air is dry. On a hot, dry day, perspiration evaporates quickly and your body is always dry. But if the air on a hot day is very moist, perspiration tends to stay on your body and you feel wet and uncomfortable.

What causes evaporation? It is heat which causes the water to evaporate or disappear into the air. All day long, water from ponds, rivers, lakes, oceans, puddles, plants and animals is heated by the sun and evaporates. The hotter it is, the quicker the water evaporates. You can test this by taking two saucers of the same size and putting a spoonful of water in each one. Place one saucer where it is warm and the other where it is cool. The water in the warmer place will dry up first. The water in this saucer has evaporated.

Wind helps to speed evaporation. If you blow on a wet piece of paper, or hold it out in the wind, it dries more

Water evaporates faster when it is spread over a large surface than when it is contained in a small area.

Water molecules from the grass and soil will evaporate and form water vapor in a glass which has been placed upside down on the grass on a sunshiny day.

THE WATER CYCLE

What makes your window cloud up?

WHEN you take a water glass and place it upside down on the grass while the sun is shining brightly, something happens to that glass. A watery film begins to form on its sides. The outside of the glass is dry, but if you run your finger around the inside, you will find that it is wet. Molecules of water from the grass and soil have evaporated. They have become water vapor. Some of these vapor molecules have been cooled and slowed down as they hit against the side of the glass. Tens of thousands of them have joined together to form fine drops of water.

The same thing happens in a car on a cold day. Your warm breath strikes the cold windshield and the molecules stick to the windshield in the same kind of watery film. Have you ever seen this happen to the windows of your house on a cold day? And did any of the drops ever get so big that they ran down the windowpane? Perhaps you have seen this happen to a glass of ice water or a cold bottle of soda.

Does water go round in circles?

But if water keeps evaporating all the time, why doesn't everything dry up? Everything doesn't dry up because of a weather system called the water cycle.

Your experiment with the glass placed upside down on the grass helps tell you where the water goes.

The first step in the water cycle is called evaporation. Water from soil and grass *evaporated* inside your glass. The second step is *condensation*. Condensation happens when water vapor begins to form tiny drops which we can see as fog or clouds. A cloudy film *condensed* on the inside of your glass. The third step is called *precipitation*. Precipitation takes place when water returns to earth in the form of rain or snow. As larger drops form in your glass, they may become large enough to fall back to the ground. If this happens, it is "raining" inside your glass.

The three steps in the water cycle are evaporation, condensation and precipitation. The sun heats the water. Water vapor rises and forms clouds. The water returns to earth when it rains.

TINY SPECKS OF MANY THINGS

What floats in the air invisibly?

IF YOU look around the room you are in, the air might look very clear to you. But there are millions of tiny specks in the air you do not see. You would need a microscope to see most of them. Smoke from factory chimneys, pollen from flowers, salt spray and ordinary household dust all help fill the air with these tiny specks. Next time you see sunlight streaming through your window, look into the stream of light. This is the air you thought was clear. Just look at the number of small particles floating in that stream. What have all these specks to do with weather?

The air is full of specks, which you can see in a beam of sunlight streaming through a window.

WHAT IS A CLOUD?

Can you see water in the air when it isn't raining?

WHEN air becomes cooler, water vapor condenses around the little specks in the air you saw in the stream of sunlight. Millions and millions of tiny droplets, like the one which made the film of water on the inside of the glass, are formed. But now the watery film is high above you in the sky. Millions of these droplets, too small to fall, cluster together in groups. These are the clouds we see in the sky. Sometimes the clouds look fat and puffy because the sun is shining through them, making them white and bright. Perhaps you have tried to pick out different shapes or imagine cloud pictures as they float by.

Sometimes the sky looks like one big cloud. This is because there are so many layers of clouds that they block out part of the sun's rays. The day is gray and cloudy.

Sometimes when clouds form very, very high in the sky, where it is much colder, these droplets freeze. Then these tiny bits of ice float in the air and look like wispy ribbons from where you watch them.

Condensation takes place when water vapor rises and forms tiny drops which we can see as clouds.

Can you walk through a cloud?

But when water droplets form at ground level, these clouds are called fog. You are walking through a cloud when you walk through fog, and you can feel the dampness of these tiny droplets on your hands and face.

On a very cold day, you form a little cloud every time your moist breath hits the cold air.

Clouds are made of millions of tiny drops of water which float in the air.

DEW AND FROST

When does dew form? AT NIGHT, when the soil, rocks and plants cool off, the layer of air which hugs the ground is cooled, too. Water vapor in the cooled air condenses as it touches the cooler soil and rocks and makes them wet. Tiny drops of water form on blades of grass and other plants. These tiny drops are dewdrops. If you get up early in the morning, you can see dewdrops sparkling in the sun. You must get up very early to see them, because when the air grows warmer, the dew evaporates and disappears into the air.

What is frost? On very cold nights the water vapor condenses directly into ice crystals. The crystals form a white film on the ground and this film is frost.

You can make your own frost. Soak the label off a gallon paint can and pack the can with alternating layers of crushed ice and rock salt. Put in four cups of ice and then two cups of rock salt. Keep repeating this layer of ice and layer of rock salt until the can is full. Now let it stand and watch what happens. Some of the water vapor in the air will condense directly into ice crystals and form a thin layer of white frost all over the outside of the can. This is the way ice cream is chilled in home freezers.

Crushed ice and rock salt are the ingredients you need in order to make frost. Frost occurs when water vapor changes into little ice crystals.

WHAT COMES OUT OF THE SKY?

Why does it rain?

HOW hot or cold the air is makes a big difference in what kind of weather comes out of the sky.

It takes only a little increase in the temperature of the air to make a cloud disappear. The droplets of water evaporate and can no longer be seen. But if the air gets colder, larger drops are formed. When they become too heavy to float in the air, they fall to earth, just as the drops of water did when they ran down inside your glass. This is rain.

Is snow frozen rain?

When the air high in the sky cools very quickly, the water vapor condenses directly into crystals and you have a snowstorm. It is not true that snow is frozen rain. Snow is water vapor which condenses directly into ice crystals, the same way ice crystals formed on the can packed with ice and salt.

Do you know that every snowflake that falls is different from every other snowflake except for one thing? Every snowflake has six sides. No two are ever alike in design except for the six sides or points. Try to examine snowflakes. Look at them through a magnifying glass. They're even prettier seen this way than they are when you watch them falling silently on a winter day.

What should you call frozen rain?

When rain or partly melted snow freezes as it falls to earth, it is called sleet. Rain freezes into hard, clear little pellets of ice and the partly melted snow freezes into soft, milky pellets.

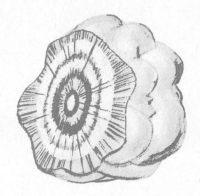

This cross-section of a hailstone shows its layers.

Of what are hailstones made? There is something else which starts in the sky as one thing and lands on earth as something else. It is hail. Hail starts as rain, but before the drops of water can fall very far, the wind blows them high up in the air where it is colder. They freeze and start to fall again. Over and over they fall and are blown back again. Each time they fall, a new layer of water vapor condenses on them, and each time they are blown up into the freezing layer of air, this new layer of water turns to ice. Finally, the stone becomes too heavy to be lifted by the wind, and it falls to earth. Some hailstones have fallen which were as large as baseballs, but usually they are not much bigger than a small pea.

Next time you are in a hailstorm, pick up a few pieces of hail and cut them in half. Inside, you can see the layers that were formed as the hailstones fell, collected more moisture and were swept back up into the freezing air again. If you count the layers, you can tell how many trips each hailstone made before it finally fell and you picked it up.

A snowflake is either a single ice crystal or made up of many crystals. In the center of each flake, there is a tiny particle, usually a speck of dust.

FIREWORKS IN THE SKY

Can you identify a thundercloud?

WHEN the sun shines and there is a cool breeze blowing, this is one of weather's pleasant faces. But just as you sometimes frown, weather has its "frowning faces," too. One of these, which you see quite often in summertime, and occasionally in the winter, is the thunderstorm. It's noisy and loud and wet, but it can be just as exciting to watch from a safe place as Fourth of July fireworks.

A thundercloud is usually one which is flat on the bottom and towers in the sky with a top shaped something like an anvil. Strong currents of air range up and down as sudden winds warn us that the storm is about to break.

What causes lightning?

Lightning is electricity — the kind which sometimes causes a shock when you shuffle your feet on a carpet and then touch something made of metal, like a doorknob or a key.

As water droplets are rubbed and pulled about, they are charged with electricity. Suddenly the electric charge in one part of a cloud is attracted to a charge in another part of the same cloud or in another cloud. As it shoots through the air, it causes the air to glow

A thundercloud. Note the flat bottom and the top part which looks like a blacksmith's anvil.

for an instant and we see a lightning flash.

You can make your own lightning. All you need are two small balloons shaped like sausages. Blow them up and tie knots in the ends. Now you are ready to make lightning, but you must do this experiment in a room which is completely dark.

Rub the balloons back and forth against your trousers or dress, or the covering of a chair or sofa. Rub both balloons at the same time. Then bring them together so that they almost touch. You will see small flashes of light as the electricity jumps between the balloons and you will hear a faint crackle. You can do this over and over again.

Try making your own lightning with two balloons by following the directions on this page.

The powerful heat from lightning causes the great air or shock waves called thunder.

What causes thunder? Outdoors, when electric currents flash through the air, the air is heated and expands rapidly. This sets a giant air wave in motion which we hear a few moments later as the roar of thunder. But light travels so fast that you see the flash at once, even before you hear the clap of thunder.

Since it takes sound about five seconds to travel one mile, you can tell how many miles you are from the lightning by dividing by five the number of seconds it takes from the time you see the lightning until you hear the thunder. For example, if you hear the thunder four seconds after you see the lightning, the flash occurred just 4/5 of a mile away.

THE STORM WITH AN EYE

THERE is another storm which is much more dangerous than a thunderstorm. You wouldn't like to be caught in this storm because it does a great deal of damage before it fades away. It is called a hurricane.

Where do hurricanes come from?

Hurricanes are storms born over tropical waters. The blazing sun beats down on the ocean waters day after day and the air above this water grows very hot. Suddenly cold air moves in from many directions. It pushes this hot air straight up until the hot air reaches a cool layer of air. The water vapor condenses very suddenly and becomes a driving rain. Cooler air from the outside moves in, in a whirling motion, like water going down a drain. The center or "eye" of the hurricane is calm, but all around it the winds and rain are swirling.

How strong is a hurricane?

Hurricanes last for several days as the storm whirls onward in its fury. It creates enormous waves which flood the land and the winds are strong enough to knock houses into a pile of wood and tear big trees up by the roots.

Cold air moving in from many directions, as the arrows indicate, is a step in the formation of a hurricane.

SKY PICTURES

What changes the way the sky looks? THE SKY around you is like a giant picture which keeps changing as the weather changes.

Sometimes the picture has a blue sky with large white clouds floating peacefully through space.

Sometimes the picture is a dark one with deep gray clouds and rain.

Sometimes the sky picture is a sunrise like a red glow in the early morning.

You watch a different picture when you watch the sun set in the west among purple clouds. Each sunset is different. Your picture changes every day.

Where must the sun be when you look at a rainbow? Once in a while, almost like a special occasion, you'll see a rainbow in your sky picture. If the sun shines through the clouds while it is still raining, as it sometimes does in summer showers, a band of many colors seems to bend across the sky. You'll miss seeing it if you face the sun. A rainbow can only be seen if the sun is at your back.

If you'd like to make tiny rainbows of your own, you might dip the top of a soda bottle into soapy water so that a film forms across the opening. Take the bottle into the sunlight so that light passes through the curved glass and strikes the soapy film. Can you see lots of colors? These are rainbow colors.

WEATHER INSTRUMENTS

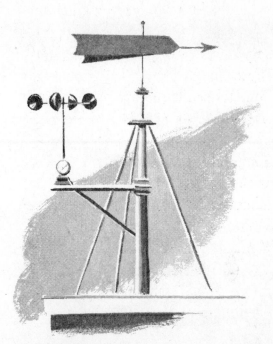

THERMOMETER: When mercury in the bulb at the bottom of the thermometer tube becomes hotter, it expands and rises up the glass tube. As it cools, it contracts and drops down. The numbers on the scale show the temperature in degrees.

ANEMOMETER: The cups "catch" the wind and spin at varying speeds, faster or slower, depending upon the wind's speed.

WIND VANE: It is used to find the direction of the wind. The arrow points to the direction from which the wind is coming. This direction gives the wind its name.

ANEROID BAROMETER: It is used to measure atmospheric pressure. A needle is connected to an airless metal box. Air pressure on the top of the box moves the needle.

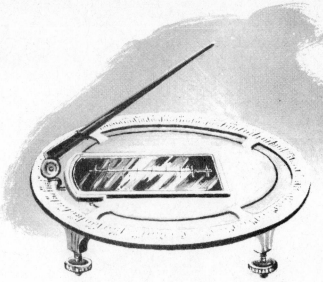

CLOUD DIRECTION INDICATOR (NEPHOSCOPE): This shows the direction of clouds by reflection. The direction of the wind high in the sky is often different from the direction of the wind near the ground.

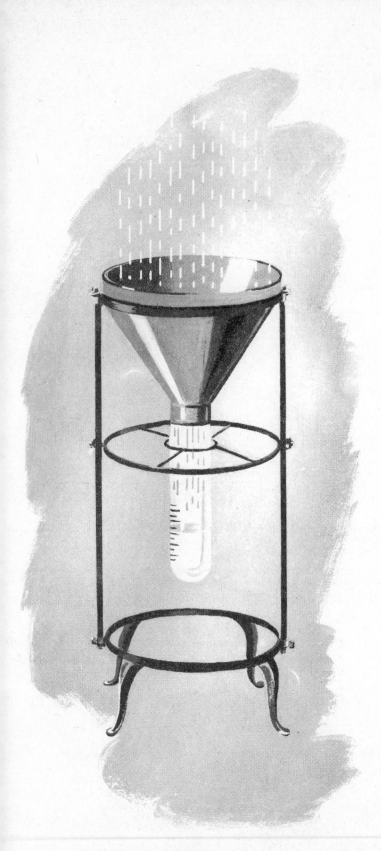

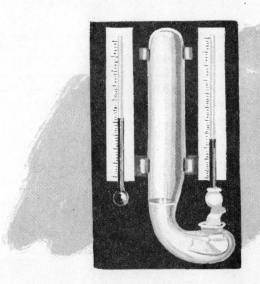

RAIN GAUGE: It measures the amount of rainfall. A wide opening catches the rain and funnels it into a narrow tube so that small amounts can be read easily.

HYGROMETER: A moist cloth is wrapped around the bulb of a thermometer. The moisture content of the air is measured by the rate of evaporation, which cools the thermometer. An ordinary dry bulb thermometer and a chart are used to determine relative humidity.

CLIMATE

IN THIS book you have been reading about the types of weather in the northern hemisphere, where you live, because this weather makes our climate. But different parts of the world have different weather. They are in different climates. You know how important weather is to you and the way you live. It's important to other people, too, who live in other places. And it is important to the plants and animals that grow and live in these places.

Here is the earth sliced in two, with bands drawn to show the different climates. One side shows the plants that grow and the other side shows the animals living in these different climates.

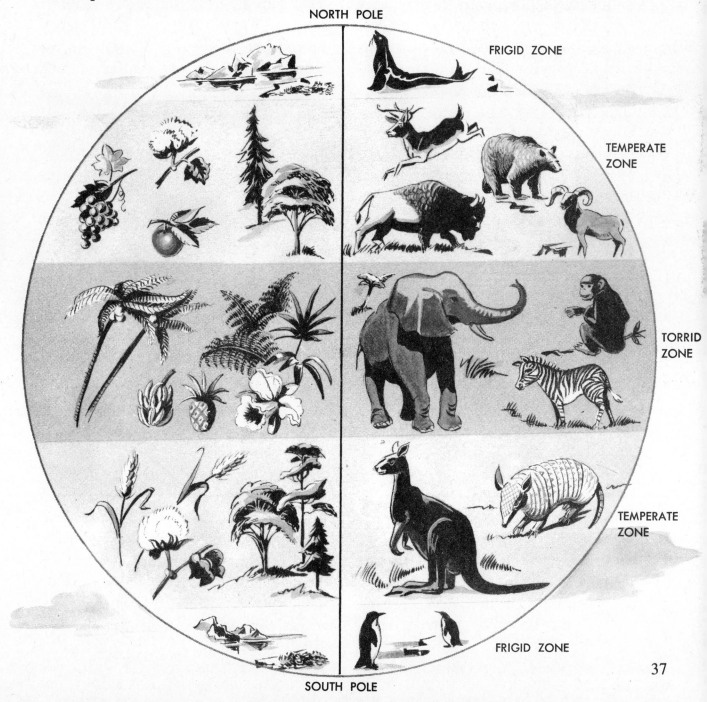

NORTH POLE

FRIGID ZONE

TEMPERATE ZONE

TORRID ZONE

TEMPERATE ZONE

FRIGID ZONE

SOUTH POLE

TYPES OF CLOUDS

CUMULUS

Cumulus is a Latin word which means "heap." These puffy white clouds heap up in thick masses. Shaped like a dome on the top and flat on the bottom, they look like mountains in the sky. Cumulus clouds often form on hot summer afternoons and are usually 4,000 to 5,000 feet above the earth. When they become thick and heavy with water, cumulus clouds may develop into thunderheads or thunderclouds, so that the presence of many of them in the sky may often mean that it is going to rain.

CIRRUS

Cirrus is a Latin word which means "curl" or "ringlet." Cirrus clouds, forming high in the sky, are feathery wisps of curly white ice crystals. These delicate clouds, which appear in dry weather, form at an altitude of from five to ten miles above the ground. They are the highest clouds in the sky and move along rapidly on the winds. Cirrus clouds are often storm warnings.

STRATUS

Stratus is also a Latin word and means "spreading out." This describes the great width of these foglike clouds. They appear at low altitudes, generally ranging from 2,000 to 7,000 feet. Spread out in calm flat layers, stratus clouds often mean bad weather ahead.

NIMBUS

Nimbus is a Latin word meaning "rainstorm," and so, nimbus clouds are rain clouds. These dark gray clouds do not have any definite shape and appear at low altitudes over a wide area of the sky.

Weather scientists use these names to describe the main cloud formations. They also use combinations of these words, such as *cirro-stratus, strato-cumulus* and *cumulo-nimbus. Cirro-stratus,* for example, means a spread-out layer of cirrus clouds. People who study weather use other words to classify clouds, such as the word *alto,* which means "high." The combinations *alto-stratus* or *alto-cumulus,* for example, tell us how high these clouds are.

THE BEAUFORT SCALE

MANY years ago, before modern weather instruments were used, a man named Sir Francis Beaufort made up a scale to describe the force of winds by the way they acted over land and sea. Here is a form of this scale. How many of these wind effects have you felt? Scale numbers indicate wind strength.

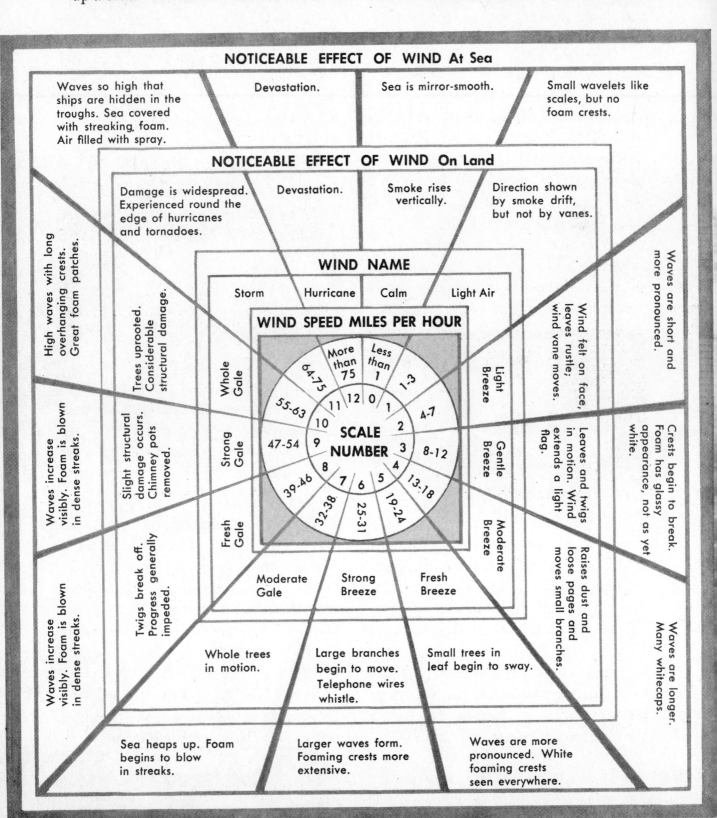

MORE WEATHER EXPERIMENTS

1. If you tried turning a glass upside down and pushing it straight down into a bowl of water as suggested on page 6, you might now try these experiments.

(a) Push your handkerchief to the bottom of a dry glass. Turn the glass upside down (making sure that the handkerchief stays in place), and push it straight down into a bowl of water. Be sure that the bowl holds enough water to cover the glass completely. You can prove that air keeps the water out, because your handkerchief will still be dry.

(b) Do the same experiment except that, instead of a handkerchief, a cork can be floated on the water in the bowl. When you press the open mouth of the glass down into the water, the pocket of air will force the cork to the bottom. As long as the glass is full of air, the water can't get in. You can use this simple science experiment as a trick. Ask a friend if he knows how to make the cork go to the bottom of the bowl without touching it. When he says that it can't be done — show him that it can!

(c) If you push an upside-down glass straight down into your bowl of water and then tilt it slightly, some of the air will get out and bubble up to the surface. Now try another stunt. Use a large pan of water, such as a dishpan, and push into it two upside-down glasses, until both are completely under water. Tilt one glass so that all of the air bubbles to the surface. One glass will now be full of water, and the other full of air. Raise them so that the open ends of the glasses remain beneath the water, but most of the glasses are out of it, as shown in the picture. Then move the glass full of air so that an edge is under the glass full of water, tipping it so that the air bubbles up into the glass full of water. As the air from one glass bubbles into the other, the glass full of water will become filled with air and the glass which was filled with air will now be filled with water. If you are careful, you can keep pouring the air back and forth from one glass to the other. The glass may be filled with either air or water, but not both. Air, like water, is real, and two real things cannot fill the same space at the same time.

2. On page 7 you discovered that air has weight — the weight of a column of air several miles high. We call this weight "pressure" and it pushes in all directions. Here are a few more experiments to show how this works.

(b) Hold a straw in your hand. Like the pressure within your body, the air pressure inside the straw is the same as the pressure on the outside. Now cut out a piece of paper about one inch square. Hold it against one end of the straw and suck through the other end. As long as you keep sucking, the paper will remain in place at the end of the straw, even after you remove your hand. The reason this happens is that as you suck air from the straw, the inside air pressure becomes less than that outside the straw. The outside pressure pushing the paper at the end of the straw holds it in place.

(a) Cut from a cereal box (or any lightweight cardboard) a piece large enough to cover the top of a drinking glass. Fill the glass with water. Holding the card tightly on top of the glass, turn the glass upside down. Then hold on to the glass with one hand and take the other hand away from the card. What makes the card stay in place and hold the water in the glass? It is the pressure of the air which pushes out in every direction. If you hold the glass sideways, the card still stays on. (It is best to do this experiment over a sink or tub, just in case of accident.)

(c) Next use the straw to drink from a glass of water. What happens? As you suck on the straw, the pressure inside the straw becomes less than the pressure pushing down against the water, and so it pushes the water up through the straw and into your mouth.

(d) Take the same straw and hold a finger over one end. Push the other end straight down into a glass of water. You will see a little water go up into the straw from the bottom as the air in the straw compresses a little. But it will not keep going up into the straw. As with the upside-down glass which was pushed straight down into the water in experiment 1(a), the water cannot enter the straw while the air is kept in. Now take your finger away from the end of the straw and you will see the water rise into the straw until it reaches the level of the rest of the water in the glass. When this hap-

pens, some of the air inside the straw is pushed out through the top. Place your finger on the end of the straw again and lift the straw out of the glass. The water will stay in the straw. No air can come in the top and the air pressing up at the bottom is strong enough to hold the water in. When you take away your finger again, the air presses down from the top with as much force as it presses up from the bottom and the weight of the water causes it to drop from the straw. The same method is used with larger glass tubes for removing tiny fish and other objects from tanks of water. Such tubes are called "dip tubes."

3. On page 9 you learned how molecules move about. High up, where the air is thinner, there are fewer molecules to bump against each other and heat up. Nearer to the earth, where the molecules are squeezed close together, they collide more often and become hotter. Try this experiment to show what happens.

(a) Fill a balloon with dried navy beans. Then blow it up and hold it at the neck so that the air cannot escape. Shake the balloon lightly. The beans will bounce about like air molecules which are always on the move. As they bounce back and forth, they will bump into one another and you will hear a little click. The more beans you are able to squeeze into the balloon before it is blown up, the more clicks there will be. And so you can see how molecules of air, squeezed together close to the earth, rub against each other more often — and how they become hotter, as the molecules of your skin do when you rub your hands back and forth quickly.

4. The fact that dark colors absorb more heat than light colors was explained on page 10. Try another experiment to prove this scientific principle.

(a) Use two white paper drinking cups. Paint one of them black. Fill both with water of the same temperature and place them in the sun. After thirty to forty minutes, test the temperature of the water in each one. (An ordinary weather or cooking thermometer will do for this purpose.) Which is warmer?

5. Air expands when it is heated. This is shown by the experiment described on page 16. Here is another interesting experiment to show that this is so.

(a) Snap the neck of a balloon around an empty quart-sized soda bottle. Since there will be very little air in the balloon, it will droop to one side. Run water from the cold water tap against the side of the bottle. Even the little bit of air which was in the balloon will seem to leave it and it will be even limper than it was in the beginning. Next, run hot water against the side of the bottle and the balloon will begin to expand with air. No air could either enter or leave the balloon. What happened? The answer is that air takes up less space when it is cold and more space when it is hot. The cold water cooled the air inside the bottle so that it took up less space than when the balloon was first put over the neck of the bottle. The hot water then heated the air in the bottle so that it took up more room and caused the air to force its way into the balloon which was able to stretch.

Hot air is lighter than cold air and therefore rises. But then, does cold air fall? Try this experiment.

(b) Get a small piece of dry ice and place it carefully in a shallow saucer of water near the edge of a table. Cold air will bubble from the saucer and you can watch it drop down to the floor. It is because cold air falls that it is possible to leave freezers uncovered in supermarkets.

6. Whether it is inside a house, as you read about on page 17, or the tornadoes and winds you read about on pages 18-20, hot air always rises and cold air comes in to take its place. You can show how this happens in a simple kitchen experiment.

(a) Sometime when your mother is using the burners on the stove, make sure that the windows and doors to the kitchen are closed. Open the door of the refrigerator and ask your mother to hold a burning match or candle at the bottom of the refrigerator opening. Notice that the cold air is falling from the refrigerator and carries the smoke down. Next, ask her to hold the match or candle halfway between the refrigerator and the stove, about a foot from the floor. Can you see the smoke moving in the direction of the stove? Now ask your mother to hold the match or candle over the stove. Watch the smoke go straight up. You have followed the course of a little breeze which you made in your own kitchen.

7. You read on pages 21 and 22 about evaporation. Your mother is especially interested in evaporation when she has clothes to dry. You can do some more experiments to find out when evaporation works best.

(a) Soak two handkerchiefs in water and hang them up to dry — one where it is sunny and the other in the shade. Which dries first?

(b) Soak two handkerchiefs in water and hang them up to dry — one open and one folded twice. Which dries first?

THE WEATHER—SEEN FROM SPACE

MANY man-made satellites have been put into orbit around the earth since the Space Age began. Of these, a good number have been weather satellites, designed to provide meteorologists — the scientists who study weather and climate — with an overall picture of atmospheric conditions. The information received, in turn, enables them to forecast the weather in specific areas with greater accuracy and to warn people of impending storms.

The first of the orbiting satellites to send weather information back to earth was the *Vanguard II,* launched on February 17, 1959. On April 1, 1960, *Tiros I* was launched — it was the first satellite to actually take pictures of the earth's weather in detail. *Tiros II,* launched on November 23 of the same year, measured infrared rays given off by the earth and also took weather pictures. And *Tiros III,* launched on July 12, 1961, was the first one to discover a hurricane — Hurricane Esther — over the Atlantic Ocean. Early warnings went out to those in the storm's probable path.

Further developments came about with the launchings of subsequent *Tiros* satellites, including the measurement of temperature and electron density in space. (The launching of *Tiros X,* in the summer of 1965, concluded this particular series.)

Another hurricane—Hurricane Dora — was progressively tracked off the coast of Florida by *Nimbus I,* a weather satellite launched on August 28, 1964. *Nimbus II* (launched May 15, 1966) measured the earth's heat balance.

The need for a world-wide network of trained weather observers who would join together in a program leading to improved weather forecasts and, eventually, weather control, was recognized by President John F. Kennedy in a speech before the United Nations on September 25, 1961.

An appropriate plan was drawn up, and by the following summer, the World Weather Watch, directed by the World Meteorological Organization (WMO), an agency of the United Nations, came into being.

The purposes of the World Weather Watch include keeping the earth's atmosphere under observation, transmitting weather information to all nations, and improving forecasting services. In the United States, the facilities of the Environmental Science Services Administration (ESSA), of which the Weather Bureau is an important part, are charged with this responsibility. The Tiros Operational Satellite (TOS) system began in February, 1966, with the launching of *ESSA I,* a weather satellite that photographs clouds, stores the information on magnetic tape, and then telemeters it to ground stations, where it is "fed" directly to a computer. The computer is capable of reproducing a picture of the cloud pattern as it then exists over all the world. The following TOS satellite, *ESSA II,* was equipped with an automatic picture-transmission system that sent pictures to receiver-recorders on the ground every 208 seconds.

Other specialized weather satellites are the Applications Technology Satellites (shortened to ATS). *ATS-I* was launched on December 6, 1966, its speed adjusted to the speed of the earth at the equator so that it remains over the same position on earth, in this case, over the Line Islands in the Pacific Ocean. It is equipped with a device which works like a camera, but which is more accurately a "pinhole-type" scanning telescope that transmits electronic pulses (translated from observed cloud formations) to a computer on the ground. A more sophisticated ATS, *ATS-III,* was launched and positioned over the Amazon River in Brazil on November 5, 1967. It transmits color pictures of half the earth every thirty minutes.

The Global Atmospheric Research Program (GARP) is another international project that will pursue greater meteorological knowledge throughout the 1970's. Balloons, buoys, satellites and airplanes will all gather information which will be computer processed at such a fast rate that long-range predictions of the weather will be both accurate and reliable. This will come about as scientists learn more about the interaction of air with the land and the oceans, and about the physics of our atmosphere that gains and loses heat by radiation.